# Hamsters

## Susan Meredith

Designed by Joe Pedley
Edited by Fiona Watt

Illustrated by Christyan Fox
Photographs by Tim Flach and Howard Allman
Cover design by Amanda Gulliver
Additional research by Jonathan Sheikh-Miller

## CONTENTS

2  What is a hamster?
4  Types of hamsters
6  Hamster homes
8  What will I need?
10  Buying a hamster
12  Feeding your hamster
14  Feeding fresh food
16  Keeping clean
18  What does it mean?
20  Taming your hamster
22  Coming out to play
24  Making a run
26  Cleaning out
28  Hamster babies
30  Going away
31  Keeping healthy
32  Index

Consultants: Anne Dray and David Baglin

# What is a hamster?

Hamsters are small, furry creatures which live wild in parts of Asia and Europe. In captivity, they make good pets, provided they are well looked after.

Hamsters are attractive and amusing to watch. They can be tamed easily, if you handle them gently and patiently. In this book you will find out all about hamsters, so that you can enjoy caring for one as a pet.

*Hamsters have rounded ears and bright, beady eyes.*

*A hamster twitches its nose and whiskers when it is curious.*

*Hamsters' strong front paws have four toes and a kind of thumb.*

*The back paws have five toes.*

*This is a type of hamster you might buy as a pet.*

## Hamster relations

*Hamsters gnaw at things. This stops their front teeth from getting too long.*

Hamsters are related to mice and gerbils. They all belong to an animal family called rodents. Rodents have front teeth which continue to grow all through their life.

## Night life

SNIFF...
SNIFF...

*You can try to train your hamster to get up in the early evening.*

Hamsters are nocturnal. This means that they sleep in the day and get up at night. This may be because in the wild there are fewer enemies around at night.

For a link to a website where you can explore a
fun and interactive guide to hamsters, go to
**www.usborne-quicklinks.com**

## Hearing

Hamsters have very good hearing and
do not like sudden or loud noises. Your
hamster will soon learn to recognize you
by the sound of your voice.

## Eyesight

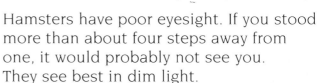

Hamsters have poor eyesight. If you stood
more than about four steps away from
one, it would probably not see you.
They see best in dim light.

## Smelling

Hamsters recognize
things by how they
smell rather than
how they look. Your
hamster will know
you by your smell as
well as your voice.

## Whiskers

A hamster uses its
whiskers as feelers.
They tell it if an
object is nearby,
or if a space is
wide enough to
get through.

*This hamster
measured the
tube with its
whiskers before
crawling through.*

# Types of hamsters

You may be able to choose from different types of hamsters when you are buying your pet. The most common pet hamster is the Syrian hamster. The other types are all known as dwarf hamsters, because they are so small.

## Syrian hamsters

Syrian hamsters can be short-haired or long-haired. You may hear them called golden hamsters. They all used to be golden, but now come in other shades too.

*Below is a long-haired Syrian. Long-haired Syrians are sometimes called teddy bears because they look so cuddly.*

*This is a short-haired Syrian. Short-haired Syrians look smaller than long-haired because they have less fur.*

## Historic hamsters

Syrian hamsters were once thought to be extinct. Then, in 1930, a nest of 11 babies and their mother were discovered in some wheatfields in Syria. Syrian hamsters first became popular as pets in America.

# Dwarf hamsters

Dwarf hamsters are less than half the size of Syrians and so can be a little more awkward to handle.

Campbell's Russian, or Djungarian, hamsters are by far the most common type of dwarf to be kept as pets.

You may see two other types of dwarf hamster in pet shops. They are called Winter White, or Siberian, hamsters and Chinese hamsters.

*This is a Campbell's Russian, or Djungarian, hamster.*

*This is a Winter White, or Siberian, hamster. In the snowy winters of Siberia, this type of hamster's fur turns white so its enemies cannot see it.*

*Chinese hamsters, like the one above, look a little like mice. They have longer tails than other hamsters.*

# One or two?

Syrian hamsters like to live alone, because this is how they live in the wild. You must keep a Syrian hamster in a cage on its own.

Dwarf hamsters live in family groups in the wild. You may be able to keep two dwarfs together, unless they fight.

# Hamster homes

Before you buy a hamster, you will need to decide what type of cage you want. Your hamster needs as big a cage as possible, so it has plenty of room to run around and play.

## Bar cages

If the cage has bars, the hamster can use them for climbing and gnawing. Bar cages also allow the hamster to get plenty of air. You can find out about the things shown inside this cage on pages 8-9.

For dwarf hamsters, the bars of the cage must be no more than 9mm ($\frac{3}{8}$in) apart, or the hamsters may squeeze through.

*The cage should have some horizontal bars, so the hamster can use them like the rungs on a ladder.*

*If a cage has more than one level, your hamster can run up and down the ladders and climb.*

*Look for a cage with a deep-sided tray at the bottom. This helps to stop the hamster from pushing out wood shavings (see page 8).*

*Make sure the doors fasten securely. Hamsters are very good at escaping.*

## Nest

In their burrows, hamsters sleep safely right out of sight. Your hamster will probably like to sleep in a special house or nest in its cage. Check that the house will still be big enough when your hamster is full grown.

*Your hamster may take its bedding into its nest.*

## Exercise wheel

*The wheel should be solid, so the hamster can't get its legs trapped.*

*A long-haired Syrian will need a large wheel.*

In the wild, hamsters may run several miles a night in search of food. Your hamster needs a wheel to get exercise. Fix it close to the bars of the cage, so the hamster can't get trapped behind it.

## Toys

*Hamsters enjoy toilet roll and paper towel tubes as much as bought toys.*

You can buy hamster toys. Don't clutter up the cage with them, though. Try putting them out for your hamster when it is running free (see page 22). Never try to force your hamster to play with a toy.

# Buying a hamster

It is best to buy a hamster from a pet shop that is recommended by people you know. Go to a shop where the animals look clean, where they are handled gently, and where the staff can answer your questions about them. Or, you could buy from a recommended hamster breeder.

## Which one?

You need to choose a healthy hamster, like the one below. Look for one that is lively and curious. Ask to see it handled and don't buy it if it is very frightened or bites.

*This is a healthy Syrian hamster.*

*Look for a plump body.*

*Its eyes should be bright, with no stickiness.*

*Check that its nose and mouth are dry.*

*Its bottom must be clean, under the tail.*

*Look for a thick, silky coat with no blemishes.*

*Check that the hamster walks without limping.*

## Male or female?

Both males and females make good pets. Don't buy a female from a cage with males in it. She may be pregnant. Females can become pregnant at only four weeks old and males can father babies at four weeks.

*Ask the staff to check the hamster's sex.*

For a link to a website where you can take a fun questionnaire
to see if a rodent is the right pet for you, go to
**www.usborne-quicklinks.com**

## How old?

*Baby hamsters don't usually fight, so they are kept together at the pet shop.*

Your hamster should be between five and eight weeks old when you buy it. Hamsters are easier to tame when they are young.

## Getting home

*The hamster may try to chew its way out of the box.*

Your hamster will be put in a box. Ask to take a little of its bedding for its new cage, so it will feel more at home. Go straight home.

## Settling in

*Put the box on the floor of the cage.*

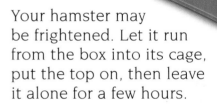

Your hamster may be frightened. Let it run from the box into its cage, put the top on, then leave it alone for a few hours.

## The ideal spot

Hamsters feel comfortable at the same temperature as humans. There are a few places where you should not put your hamster's cage. Keep it away from:
- radiators and fires
- direct sunlight
- windows and doors
- damp places
- televisions and stereos
- other pets

*You may not get much sleep, if you keep your hamster in your bedroom.*

# Feeding your hamster

To stay healthy, your hamster needs a combination of dried hamster food from a pet shop, fresh fruit and vegetables, and water. You can find out about fresh food and water on pages 14-15.

Rolled barley

Sunflower seeds

Flaked pea

Wheat

Oats

Peanuts

Alfalfa

## Dried food

Most hamster food consists of a mixture like the one shown here. This is the type of food hamsters eat in the wild. In some countries, people give special hamster pellets and food blocks too. Store the food in a cool place, in an airtight container. Don't keep it for more than three months.

Biscuits

Corn

Maize

Broad beans

Locust beans

## How much and when?

*Your hamster may learn to anticipate food.*

A hamster needs about a tablespoon of dried food mix a day. If you give pellets, ask at the pet shop what the correct amount is.

Try to feed your hamster at the same time every day, say in the early evening. It may then get used to getting up at that time.

## Hoarding food

*Hamsters often make a food store near their bed.*

In the wild, hamsters hoard their food in a store, in case supplies are hard to find later. They make food stores in their cages too.

12

## Treats

You can buy your hamster various treats. Ask at the pet shop how often you should give these.

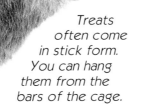

*Treats often come in stick form. You can hang them from the bars of the cage.*

## Forbidden food

There are several foods which will make a hamster unwell. Never give sweets, chocolate, salted snacks, salted nuts, or anything spicy. (See also page 14.)

## Pouches

Hamsters have big pouches, like pockets, in their cheeks. In the wild, they fill their pouches with food to carry it back to the safety of their burrow. They empty their pouches by pushing the food out with their paws.

*Your hamster will stuff its pouches with food, then carry it to the store in its cage.*

# Feeding fresh food

Hamsters need a small amount of fresh fruit or vegetables every day. You can give the fresh food at the same time as the dried hamster food. You will soon get to know which fruit and vegetables your hamster prefers. If it doesn't like something, it won't eat it.

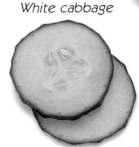

*White cabbage*

*Tomato*

*Cucumber*

*Melon*

*Apple*

*Carrot*

*Grapes*

*Hamsters usually like these foods.*

## Foods to avoid

Don't give your hamster onions, garlic, oranges or other citrus fruits. These foods can make hamsters unwell. Only give lettuce or melon in tiny amounts.

## Preparing the food

Before you give fruit or vegetables to your hamster, you need to wash them thoroughly in cold water, then dry them on paper towel. Don't peel them or take out seeds, though. Your hamster will enjoy doing this itself.

*This hamster is wrestling with a tomato.*

## How much to give

Your hamster mustn't have too much fresh fruit and vegetables, or it will get a tummy ache. Between 10 and 20g (about ½oz) a day is about the right amount. Fresh food soon goes bad, so throw away any leftovers every day.

*A hamster with a day's portion of carrot and grape.*

## Milk and yogurt

*A teaspoonful of yogurt, or about a tablespoon of milk, is enough for one day.*

*Put milk or yogurt in a heavy dish.*

Hamsters can have very fresh milk or live, natural, unsweetened yogurt. Throw leftovers away next morning and wash the dish very well.

## Water

*If bubbles rise to the top as your hamster drinks, the bottle is working.*

Give your hamster fresh water every day, but don't worry if it doesn't drink very much. It will get water from fruit and vegetables.

## Vitamins and minerals

*Extra vitamins and minerals may be useful when your hamster is old.*

You can buy vitamin drops and mineral stones for hamsters. If yours is healthy and has a good diet, it shouldn't really need them.

# Keeping clean

Hamsters are very clean. They wash themselves all over several times a day and have mini-washes at other times, too.

## Fur

A hamster's fur keeps it warm in the night-time cold. If a hamster keeps its fur neat and tidy, it will be warmer than if the fur is all tousled.

## Scent glands

Syrian hamsters have a dark patch on each hip. These are scent glands.

Hamsters let out a smelly grease from their scent glands, as they rub against things. This marks the things as their property.

## Washing routine

Hamsters wash quickly and energetically. They lick their front paws over and over again and use them as face cloths. If they can't reach a part of their body with their front paws, they use their back paws instead. Their claws make good combs.

*Hamsters use their teeth to nibble out tangles in their fur.*

*Hamsters can reach to clean even the most awkward places.*

*This hamster is washing the back of its neck.*

## Long hair tangles

Hamsters don't usually need any help with grooming. Just occasionally, a long-haired hamster may get a stubborn tangle in its fur. You can tease this out, using a bristle toothbrush or a special hamster brush.

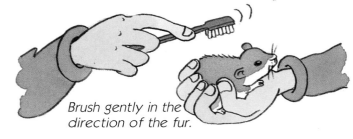

*Brush gently in the direction of the fur.*

*Don't brush the hamster's head.*

## Healthy teeth

You need to give your hamster hard things to gnaw, or its front teeth will get too long. You can try carrots, an unshelled peanut, toilet roll and paper towel tubes, or a mineral stone or special gnawing block from a pet shop.

*Gnawing helps to clean the teeth, as well as keeping their length down.*

## Open wide

YAWN!

Although you can't usually see them, hamsters have 12 teeth at the back of their mouth for chewing, as well as the 4 at the front.

*Chewing a wood gnawing block from a pet shop.*

# What does it mean?

If you watch your hamster closely, you may be able to tell how it is feeling from some of the things it does.

*This hamster has just woken up.*

## Feeling sleepy

If your hamster's ears are folded back, it is a sign that it is sleepy. Don't try to play with it or it could get annoyed and bite.

## Bed-making

Hamsters are good at making beds to suit the weather. They pile on bedding when it is cold, and spread it out when it is warm.

*A bed for cold weather*

*A bed for warm weather*

Sometimes your hamster may move its bed to a different part of its cage, just because it feels like a change.

## Toilet habits

Some hamsters are quite tidy and always pee in the same part of their cage, usually in a corner.

*If your hamster starts turning round and round, it means it wants to do a pee.*

Don't worry about your hamster keeping its droppings in its food store. It does this to show that it owns the store.

YUK!

Hamsters cannot get all the goodness they need from food the first time they eat it, so they eat their droppings to get more.

## Feeling curious

If your hamster hears or smells something interesting, it will lift one of its front paws, or stand right up on its hind legs, ready to investigate. It will listen hard and sniff the air.

*These hamsters are both curious.*

## Feeling frightened

*If a hamster screeches, it is really frightened.*

If a hamster is afraid, it may freeze quite still, or it may start washing very fast. It may creep along jerkily, its belly pressed to the ground and its tail up, or it may stand on its hind legs and bare its teeth.

## Gnawing the bars

If your hamster gnaws its cage bars, it may be bored and want to come out, or it may be trying to stop its teeth from getting too long. Try giving it something else to gnaw (see page 17) and see if it stops.

19

# Taming your hamster

If you handle your hamster gently and patiently, it should become very tame. The sooner you begin, the easier taming will be. Start the day after you buy your hamster. Then, try to handle it three or four times every day, but only for a few minutes at a time. You will need to have a grown-up to help you at first.

## Time of day

Wait for your hamster to be wide awake and active. Give it time after getting up to go to the toilet, and have a snack and perhaps a wash.

## Getting prepared

Put your hamster's cage on the floor in a quiet room. Block off the area around it so the hamster can't escape. Take off the lid.

## Introducing yourself

Talk softly to your hamster, so it gets to know your voice. Then, offer it some food from your fingers and stroke it gently, so it gets to know your smell. Keep all your movements slow and smooth. Your hamster may take a few days to get used to this.

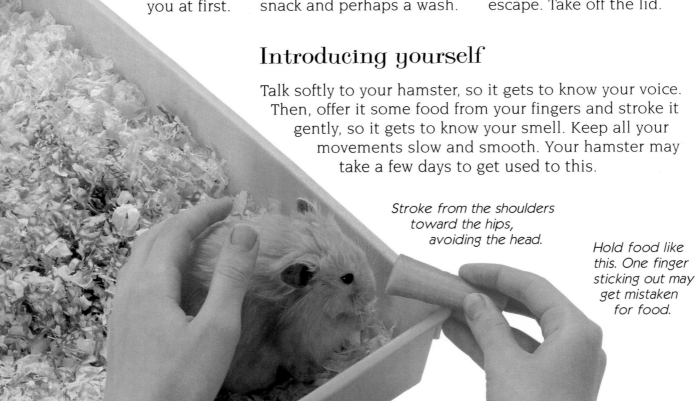

*Stroke from the shoulders toward the hips, avoiding the head.*

*Hold food like this. One finger sticking out may get mistaken for food.*

# Picking your hamster up

*Never drop your hamster. A fall from over 20cm (8in) may hurt it badly.*

1. Facing your hamster, so it can see you, cup your hands around it like this. Only lift it just off the cage floor.

*Hold your hamster securely but not too tightly, or you will hurt it.*

2. Move your hands to this position. If your hamster wriggles, let it get down and try again later.

3. Once you can pick your hamster up, take it out of its cage, and sit down to let it run from hand to hand.

4. If it runs too fast for you, block its path like this, to slow it down. It will also enjoy climbing all over you.

# Avoiding bites

Hamsters only bite if they are frightened. Never tease your hamster. Don't poke things through the bars.

Don't pick your hamster up with the smell of food on your hands. Try not to make sudden, jerky movements.

Don't shout at your hamster or punish it, even if it does bite. This will only make it more likely to bite again.

For a link to a website where you can watch a fun cartoon showing you how to pick up your hamster, go to **www.usborne-quicklinks.com**

# Coming out to play

Your hamster will keep itself busy in its cage, but it is good for it to come out to play too. Once it is tame, it will probably enjoy playing with you best of all.

## When to play

*A hamster mustn't play for too long without a rest.*

You should get your hamster out for only 10-15 minutes at a time, but you can get it out more than once in an evening. If it doesn't respond to its name and a gentle tap on the cage, let it sleep.

## Danger

*Make sure no one opens a door onto your hamster. It could be badly hurt.*

*Some furniture can't easily be moved. Don't let your hamster get into awkward gaps.*

Keep your hamster away from people's feet, other pets, hot radiators, pipes and fires, electric sockets and cables, and water it could drown in.

## Running free

Your hamster will love to explore a room. First, block off any escape routes. Watch your hamster all the time, for its own safety and to make sure it doesn't gnaw anything valuable, such as furniture. Don't let it run free like this until it is tame.

*Put out any toys you have bought for your hamster.*

## Exercise balls

You can buy special balls for hamsters to run around in. Don't keep your hamster in one of these for more than 10-15 minutes a day. Let it out sooner if it shows signs of distress, such as washing very fast.

*An exercise ball may be useful if it is not safe for your hamster to run free.*

*If the ball keeps coming open, put tape over its entrance.*

## Escapes

*Your hamster will be able to climb into the bucket but not out again.*

*Put a certain number of seeds in one corner of each room.*

If your hamster escapes, try leaving its cage open on the floor nearby. It may come back for food and then curl up in bed.

Or, put strong-smelling food, such as cabbage, in a bucket with around 2.5cm (1in) of shavings and some bedding. Make steps with books.

If you aren't sure which room the hamster is in, put sunflower seeds in each one, then shut the doors. Do any of them disappear?

For a link to a website where you can find out how to make fun toys for your hamster, go to **www.usborne-quicklinks.com**

# Making a run

You may like to make a run for your hamster to play in, when it is out of its cage. You can either copy the run shown on the right, or make a simpler one of your own. First, you will need to collect some toilet roll and paper towel tubes, and some empty tissue boxes.

## Safety first

*A pale, plain box is safest.*

Try to find pale boxes, without much printing on them. Strong dyes and print may harm your hamster if it chews the boxes.

Fit the run together without tape or glue. Tape may harm your hamster if it eats some. It is best to avoid even non-toxic glue.

Some cardboard can be stiff to cut. Ask someone to help you, if it is hard to get the point of your scissors through to start your cuts.

## Tubes into boxes

1. To fit a tube into a box, position the tube on one side of the box, then draw around the end of it.

2. Cut out the circle. It may be easiest to make a hole in the middle of the circle first, then cut to the edge.

3. Push the tube into the hole. Slope it down, or leave it straight so your hamster has to climb into it.

# Tubes into tubes

*Put only a small amount of glue on the circle.*

*For a join like this, this tube needs to be quite wide.*

1. To fit tubes together, draw around the end of one onto paper. Cut out the circle.

2. Glue the circle onto the other tube, where you want the hole. Cut the circle out.

3. Push the first tube into the hole. Leave room for your hamster to move.

# Holes and slits

Cut holes in the top of some tubes. Make sure they are big enough for your hamster to squeeze through.

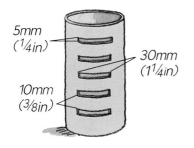

5mm (¼in)

30mm (1¼in)

10mm (⅜in)

Cut slits in a tube, for your hamster to climb up. You don't need to cut exactly to the sizes shown above.

*Hamsters enjoy rushing around in a run and popping up in different places.*

# Cleaning out

Hamsters don't like having their cages disturbed but, to stay healthy, they need to be cleaned out once a week. You will need someone to help you at first. Always wash your hands thoroughly after cleaning.

## When to clean out

You need to clean out your hamster when it is awake. If no one is around to play with it, put it in a deep, clean cardboard box, bucket or bin, while you clean.

*Put shavings in a deep bucket and let your hamster burrow.*

*Keep an eye on your hamster. It can climb out, unless there is a gap of at least 23cm (9in) between the rim and the shavings.*

## Every day

*Scoop up wet shavings with paper towel or a scoop.*

*Wrap wet shavings in newspaper and throw them away.*

Give your hamster fresh water every day, and throw away any leftover fresh food before it starts to rot. If the shavings are wet and smelly where your hamster pees, you can replace them with fresh ones.

## Emptying the cage

*Separate out some bedding and dried food.*

Empty out all the shavings, bedding and food once a week. Keep half the bedding and a little dry food from the food store. It will comfort your hamster if you put these familiar things back into its clean cage.

For a link to a website where you can send an electronic
postcard of a hamster to a friend, go to
**www.usborne-quicklinks.com**

# Washing out

*Shake the bottle
hard to loosen any
dirt around the
ball bearing.*

*Use a bottle brush
to get the bottle
really clean inside.*

Use hot water and mild dishwashing liquid
to wash the bottle, dish, house, wheel and
cage bottom. Rinse them well, then dry
them on paper towels or an old, clean tea
towel. Wash the cage bars every few weeks.

# Avoiding germs

*Clean the bathtub
or sink well, when
you've finished.*

*Only use the hamster
cleaning equipment for
your hamster's things.*

Don't clean near people's food or dishes.
You could clean in the bathroom. It's a
good idea for the hamster's things to be
disinfected every few weeks with
disinfectant used for babies' equipment.

# Settling back in

When you put your hamster back in its
clean cage, it may seem upset. It may rush
around with the fresh shavings and
bedding in its mouth. It may rub its scent
glands along the side of the cage. It may
wash a lot. Don't worry, it will
soon settle down again.

*At first, a
hamster may
refuse to
make its
bed in a
clean cage.*

27

# Hamster babies

Hamsters are born in the same way as humans. They don't hatch out of eggs like some small animals do. Their first food is milk, which they drink straight from their mothers.

Syrian hamsters usually have about eight babies at a time, and dwarfs have about five. Never try to breed hamsters yourself without expert advice.

## Newborn hamsters

Newborn hamsters have no fur. They can't see or hear, but they can smell things. They are about the same length and weight as a medium-sized paperclip.

*This is a nest of four-day-old Syrian hamsters.*

## Growing up

*The babies start sitting up to clean themselves but often topple over.*

The babies change fast. After two weeks, they have fur, and can see, hear and walk unsteadily. They start eating normal hamster food as well as their mother's milk.

## Rough and tumble

Baby hamsters tumble around and look as though they are fighting, but they are only playing. They often sleep piled on top of one another, but rarely come to any harm.

For a link to a website where you can find out a lot
more about taking care of your hamster, go to
**www.usborne-quicklinks.com**

## Leaving the nest

At three to four weeks old,
the babies have to leave
their mother. If they stay
with her for much longer,
she may attack them. Syrian
babies will probably start to fight
one another, if they stay together
for longer than a few more weeks.

## Full grown

*These Syrians
are four
weeks old.*

*This three-month-old
Syrian is now grown up.*

## One parent or two?

*A dwarf father
may carry food
to the babies.*

Syrian hamsters are full grown by the time
they are three or four months old. Dwarfs
are full grown even earlier, at about two
months old. From now on, hamsters don't
change much in appearance.

Syrian babies are looked after by their
mother only, because adult Syrians don't
live with a partner. As dwarf hamsters
often live in pairs, there may be a mother
and a father to look after the babies.

# Going away

You can leave hamsters on their own for up to two nights, because of the way they store their food. Leave an extra water bottle in the cage, if your hamster drinks a lot. Only leave enough fresh food for the first day.

If you are going away for more than two nights, someone will need to come in to feed your hamster. Better still, ask if it can stay at a friend's, or board it at a pet shop or vet's.

*Your hamster will be pleased to have a treat, while you are away.*

## Going to a friend's

*Leave your friend everything she will need.*

*Keep two hamsters in separate rooms.*

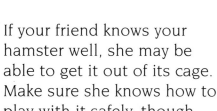

Give instructions to your friend. Say how much food to give, and which fresh foods. Explain how to clean your hamster's cage out.

If your friend knows your hamster well, she may be able to get it out of its cage. Make sure she knows how to play with it safely, though.

Your hamster mustn't play with another hamster. They will probably fight, and may mate. It is best if they can't even smell each other.

# Keeping healthy

If hamsters are well cared for, they don't often become ill. They usually live for around two years. As they get old, they start to slow down and need to sleep more. If you are ever worried about your hamster, take it to see a vet.

## Upset stomach

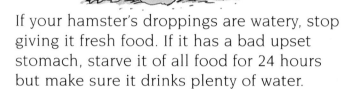

*You may need to put the water bottle to your hamster's mouth.*

If your hamster's droppings are watery, stop giving it fresh food. If it has a bad upset stomach, starve it of all food for 24 hours but make sure it drinks plenty of water.

## Frozen stiff

If your hamster appears to die in cold weather, it may just be in a very deep sleep. Don't try to wake it quickly. First, move it to a warm place. Then, hold it very gently. The warmth of your body may revive it in an hour or so. Afterwards, make sure it has plenty of extra bedding.

## On the move

If your hamster needs to see a vet, you could take it in a small pet carrier like the one in this photograph.

*A pair of dwarfs can travel together.*

# Index

babies, 10, 11, 28-29
bedding, 8, 9, 18, 26, 31
biting, 18, 21
burrows, 7, 8, 9, 13

cages, 6-7, 8
Campbell's Russian
    hamsters, 5
Chinese hamsters, 5
climbing, 6, 7, 21, 23, 25, 26

disinfecting, 27
Djungarian hamsters, 5
droppings, 18, 31
dwarf hamsters, 4, 5, 6, 7,
    28, 29, 31

exercise balls, 23
exercise wheel, 9, 27
eyesight, 3, 28

female hamsters, 10
fighting, 5, 11, 28, 29, 30
food,
    dish, 8, 27
    dried, 12-13, 26
    fresh, 14-15, 26, 30, 31

fur, 16, 28

germs, 27
gnawing, 2, 6, 17, 19, 22

health, 10, 12, 26, 31
hearing, 3, 19, 28
hoarding food, 12
holding your hamster, 21
house, 9, 27

long-haired hamsters, 4,
    9, 17

male hamsters, 10
milk, 15, 28
minerals, 15

nest, 9

peeing, 18
pouches, 13

rodents, 2

sawdust, 8
scent glands, 16, 27

short-haired hamsters, 4
Siberian hamsters, 5
sleeping, 2, 9, 18, 28, 31
smell, sense of, 3, 19, 28
storing food, 12
stroking your hamster, 20
Syrian hamsters, 4, 5, 7,
    28, 29

teddy bear hamsters, 4
teeth, 2, 16, 17, 19
toys, 9
treats, 13

vet, 30, 31
vitamins, 15

washing, 16, 19, 23, 27
water, 15, 26, 31
water bottle, 8, 15, 27
whiskers, 2, 3
wild hamsters, 2, 5, 7, 9,
    12, 13
Winter White hamsters, 5
wood shavings, 8, 26

yogurt, 15

With thanks to Armitage Brothers plc, Rosewood Pet Products Ltd and
Rolf C. Hagen (UK) Ltd for supplying hamster equipment used in photographs.
Thanks also to Jessica Bailey and Nadia Allman.